CELTIC ISLES

For Jean –
lover of island ways

CELTIC ISLES

Prayers and Meditations
from Holy Islands

Joyce Denham

LION

A Lion Book
an imprint of
Lion Hudson plc
Mayfield House, 256 Banbury Road,
Oxford OX2 7DH, England
www.lionhudson.com
ISBN 0 7459 5184 8

First edition 2005
10 9 8 7 6 5 4 3 2 1 0

A catalogue record for this book is available
from the British Library

Typeset in 10/15 GoudyOldStyle
Printed and bound in China

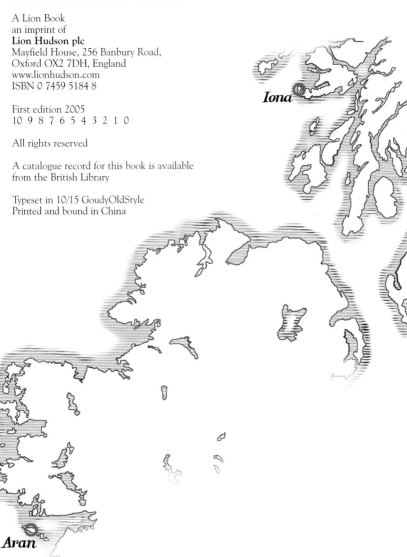

Iona

Aran

CONTENTS

Lindisfarne

pREfACE

This book is about islands. It is also about God, and us. It draws on two ancient metaphors. The first is that of the sea as God's primal enemy – an unexpected image for many of us today, for we are taught to think first of the beauty of the sea rather than its terrors. But for ancient coastal peoples who, without the advantages of scientific weather forecasting, regularly found themselves battling tempests, the sea served as a profound metaphor for everything that is against both God and us, everything that wants to destroy us. The second metaphor is that of the land as our safe habitation; it represents God's defeat of the treacherous and always-invading sea.

Islands encapsulate both these metaphors, for they are bits of safe and solid ground in the midst of seemingly un-crossable and deadly waters. The fact that islands are completely surrounded by water means that every island is, first and foremost, a refuge. All islands everywhere – small or large – declare salvation.

Ireland is an island, as is Great Britain, and off each of their jagged coastlines lie other, much smaller islands, including Aran, Iona and Lindisfarne, which feature in this book. The Celts of Ireland and Great Britain knew all about islands and island ways. For them, a solitary chunk of rock in the midst of ocean was a place to meet God. They understood the ancient metaphors of the sea as God's enemy and the land as a refuge, and their lives were determined by them. And that is what this book is all about: living as though on an island, while surrounded on all sides by the sea. Sometimes we feel that we are living in the centre of a violent storm; sometimes we enjoy a time of calm and peace; and most often we are part of the rhythmic ebb and flow of daily worldly existence. But whatever the conditions outside us, we can without fail find an island refuge deep within us. The thoughts in this book are meant to help us do that very thing – to dwell on islands of peace, even as the waves of turmoil seek to drown us.

There is more than one way to use this book. First, you could study chapters one to three to gain a deeper understanding of the two metaphors just described; the prayers and meditations in chapters four to seven are all inspired by them. Next, you could read straight through chapters four to six; or you could select a chapter according to your particular mood. For example, if you find yourself in great difficulty, or swamped by depression, or buffeted by the winds of grief or doubt, you may want to focus on chapter four and use the prayers and meditations that centre on Aran – an island subjected to the brutality of Atlantic gales. Chapter five, 'Calm of Iona', is for the calm times; and chapter six, 'Ebb and Flow of Lindisfarne', is for the predictable ebb and flow of everyday life. Finally, chapter seven is for any time. It summarizes the book's themes and makes them personal.

As you spend time in each island chapter, you'll find that the photographs are an integral part of the meditations. The beauty of each island setting is paired with specific poems and prayers. Some of the extracts are from the Bible; some are ancient Celtic prayers from an anthology called *Carmina Gadelica*; the remainder are my own compositions. The pictures and words should work together to lead you into a sacred space, where God's Spirit will meet you on your own island of quiet revelation. My hope is that you will return to this book often, and find within it a special place of retreat and prayer.

Finally, if you have the good fortune to visit in person any or all of the islands described here, this book will be the perfect companion on your pilgrimage.

Joyce Denham

1
SEA

1
shipwrecked

In the year AD 59, at a port on the eastern shore of the Mediterranean Sea, 276 men boarded a cargo ship bound for Rome. Among them just happened to be the apostle Paul. Little did these people dream that travelling with Paul would involve a brush with death, then salvation – the risk and the hope of travelling with Jesus. Paul was a prisoner in the custody of a Roman centurion named Julius, having been falsely accused of bringing a Gentile (non-Jewish) man into the Jewish-only court of the Temple in Jerusalem – a crime that carried the death penalty. This infraction meant nothing to the Romans who occupied Jerusalem, but because it was so serious to the Jews, the Romans permitted the severest punishment. Once in Rome, Paul would face trial. If found guilty, he would be executed.

Julius had the burdensome task of ensuring that Paul, and the other prisoners in his custody, made it safely to Italy, despite the treacherous sea journey required. He found an Alexandrian ship embarking for Rome and demanded passage. When they set sail from Lycia to cross the Mediterranean, winter was upon them and Paul knew they had no chance of navigating the seasonal storms. He begged Julius to remain at port and wait out the winter, but both Julius and the ship's captain ignored him. They put out to sea on the chance that they could make it to Phoenix, a harbour on the island of Crete.

Soon a violent northeaster battered the ill-fated ship. Day after day the raging storm blotted out the sun and stars. The crew flung the cargo and ship's tackle overboard and despaired of their lives; they ate nothing as they reeled and puked and cried in agony to their gods. Then Paul, the prisoner, took charge. 'If only you had listened to me,' he rebuked them, 'we would not be in these seething waters, on the brink of death! But the God whom I worship sent an angel to me last night, who told me that every man on board this ship will be saved. So take courage!'

Fourteen days had passed when the sailors sensed they were nearing land. They took soundings, measuring the depth of the sea: 120 feet (37 metres). Then again: 90 feet (27 metres). Terror seized them; surely they would be smashed on the rocks! Swiftly and secretly they readied the lifeboat for escape, which had room only for them. Let the prisoners and soldiers perish, they decided. When Paul saw what they were up to, he cried out to Julius that unless the sailors stayed with the ship, no one – not one man – would be saved. By now Julius believed him. His guards fell upon the bolting crew, cut the ropes to the lifeboat and set it adrift. Paul begged the men to take some food. No one had eaten for two weeks. 'You need strength to endure what's coming next,' he persuaded them. 'But I promise you that not one hair on your heads will be lost.' Encouraged by his confidence, the ravenous men devoured bread until they were full. And, to lighten the load, they threw the remaining cargo of grain into the sea. Then they waited.

Suddenly a mass of sheer rock seemed to rise from the depths. Were they hallucinating? 'Land!' they cried ecstatically. 'We're saved!' In the midst of this violent storm, they had encountered a gigantic island. They detected a bay, barely visible through a wall of swirling mist. At once they scrambled to raise the foresail and tried to head into the shelter, but they were nearly pitched overboard: the bow struck a sandbar and lodged there, while the pounding waves broke the stern into pieces – exactly what the sailors had feared.

'Kill the prisoners!' the guards cried in anguish. 'If they escape, it will be our bodies – not theirs – that will be nailed to crosses!'

'No!' growled Julius. 'I want them alive. I want Paul alive!'

The stronger men swam for shore; the weaker clung to planks. Over and over the powerful waves threatened to bury them. Men, scattered throughout the water, sank and resurfaced as if they were no larger than the rats fleeing the wreckage. Finally, soaked and freezing, all 276 of them were washed ashore alive, just as Paul had promised. They had found Malta.

Paul may very well have been the only Jew on board the doomed ship. Perhaps that's why the centurion paid no attention to his warnings at first. He knew that the Jewish people (the Israelites) had little experience of the Mediterranean. Historically, they were never a seafaring bunch. Their passion was for land, the land that Yahweh, their powerful and personal god, had granted them by covenant. As a Jew, Paul was unusual in that he had completed several hazardous, yet remarkably successful, sea voyages across the waters of the Roman empire. For years he had recklessly traversed both the Mediterranean and the Aegean Seas, and those often-terrifying voyages had only confirmed that his ancestors were right to fear the sea. In their imaginations, the bottomless waters were writhing with chaos monsters and dread serpents. To them, the sea was nothing less than Yahweh's most ancient and ferocious enemy. No clear-thinking Jew would ever have chosen to spend life on this cold, treacherous and briny wasteland.

2
SEA AND LAND

For us to understand an ancient Israelite's fear of the sea, and for us to grasp the significance of islands as places of deliverance from death, we must first understand the basics of both ancient near-eastern and medieval European cosmology.

Medieval cartographers typically placed east, not north, at the tops of their maps. East, or orient, means 'dawn, the source, beginnings'. These map-makers believed that the source of all life was the God of ancient Israel – the God of the Bible. Unlike the gods worshipped by the surrounding nations – nature deities who, it was believed, exercised their unpredictable and often vindictive powers only in their limited locales – Israel's God wielded power everywhere. What's more, this God was personable and knowable, and even had a special name – a first name, really, although the Israelites felt that it was too holy to utter aloud. The name is *Yahweh*. No one today knows exactly how to pronounce it, but it is something like 'yah-hway'. Its meaning is too profound to fully define, but it clearly includes the following: the One Who Is; the I Am; the Beginning and the End.

As a nation, ancient Israel existed to teach the whole world that Yahweh is the one true God – the God who is over and above all things, who is too ancient to even have an origin, who pre-existed all things everywhere, and who created and sustains all life. Which means, of course, that Yahweh *had* to be the source of the earth's beginnings – its orient. And Yahweh, according to the Israelites, sat enthroned above the sky. God, our orient, our east, was up – hence east appeared at the tops of medieval maps.

This fact was also central to how early Celtic Christians imagined

the cosmos. The Celts in Ireland converted to the Christian faith early in the fifth century, chiefly due to the radical love and service of St Patrick, a Roman Briton who was kidnapped as a teenager by Irish pirates and sold into slavery. After his escape, he returned to Ireland to serve the same people who had treated him so cruelly. It was Patrick's spiritual descendants, generations of intrepid Irish monks and nuns, who took the Christian message of God's love for humanity to Scotland, northern England and beyond. As the people of Ireland and Great Britain became Christians, they adopted the world-view set forth in the Bible. Thus they saw the universe just as any ancient Israelite would have seen it, because cosmological views had changed very little since the time of Moses. So what did an ancient Israelite, and hence a Celtic Christian, think the universe looked like? Most importantly, it was wet. It was an angry and unfathomable sea, with powerful springs rising from its depths. Thankfully, humans, along with all of the other creatures, and the plants, floated on an island of mainly dry, solid land called the earth – land that Yahweh had made. This land offered protection from the terrifying waters below. But the earth was not floating freely on the primordial sea; rather, it was anchored, perched on great pillars whose foundations were planted in the deep abyss.

In addition to the lower waters, the ancient Israelites and early

Celtic Christians believed that there were also waters above the earth. To prevent people from drowning in them, God created a huge, brass dome called the firmament, which covered the earth just like a domed glass lid covers a cheese platter. The firmament held back the massive waters above the earth. It was supported by mountains, and living beneath it people could observe how the sun came and went through gates between the mountains: entering through one gate each and every morning, and exiting through another gate each and every night. Between morning and evening, the sun travelled slowly across the great firmament, on its daily journey from entrance to exit. There were tiny holes in the firmament, through which the sun shone during the night, as stars, when it occupied the scary universe outside. Through these holes, the waters above the firmament sometimes leaked, as rain.

Above all of this – above the waters beneath the earth, above the earth itself, above the firmament over the earth, and above the waters over the firmament – floated Yahweh's glorious throne. It is this picture that the ancient Israelite poets had in mind when they composed their liturgical hymns:

The earth is the Lord's and all that is in it,
  the world, and those who live in it;
for he has founded it upon the seas,
  and established it on the rivers.
PSALM 24:1–2

The Lord sits enthroned over the flood;
  the Lord sits enthroned as king forever.
PSALM 29:10

This view of the universe was not so very different from that of the pagan nations – the Canaanites, Babylonians and Syrians – that surrounded Israel in approximately 2000 BC. They too told stories about a dark sea from which all life emerged. If we were to rewrite the Bible in the terms of ancient paganism, it would open with the line, 'In the beginning, all was water.'

But there was an extremely important difference between how the Israelites understood this water and how their neighbours understood it. That difference lies in the role played by chaos. Pagan creation myths speak of a formless, primordial sea inhabited by gods who took the shape of chaos monsters. These were frightening and extremely self-centred beings, and they were, not surprisingly, based upon the worst kinds of humans. These gods sometimes engaged in sex, but more often they waged war against one another. At some point within this watery chaos, the earth was formed – literally out of one or more of these gods. In other words, creation sprang from the gods themselves – from their very bodies. In one story, the chief goddess splits in two, like a clam shell. Her upper shell holds back the waters above, and her lower shell holds back the waters beneath, so that earth can exist in the dry space within her clam-shell body.

This, basically, is the cosmological view that Abraham, the father of the Israelite nation, would have been taught as a child: that the earth arose out of the body of a water-dwelling chaos monster. When he reached manhood, however, Abraham's view changed radically, so radically that he is regarded as the first monotheist. In some amazing, world-view changing, earth-shattering event, Abraham met Yahweh, the Lord of sea and land, maker of all that exists, the one true God whose name is I Am. The Bible of Abraham's descendants opens with the line, 'In the beginning, God created the heavens and the earth.' In this creation account, the world does not arise out of the body of a chaos monster. Instead, God – who is the opposite of chaos – makes the world, speaking it into existence. The earth is separate from God; it is God's handiwork. In fact, God even makes the sea itself, for nothing exists apart from God:

For the Lord is a great God,
  and a great King above all gods.
In his hand are the depths of the earth;
  the heights of the mountains are his also.
The sea is his, for he made it,
  and the dry land, which his hands have formed.
PSALM 95:3–5

In the following passage, the writer of Proverbs describes God as pre-existing everything. Wisdom personified is the speaker in this poem about all the things that Yahweh made:

When there were no depths I was brought forth,
  when there were no springs abounding with water.
Before the mountains had been shaped,
  before the hills, I was brought forth –
when he had not yet made earth and fields,
  or the world's first bits of soil.
When he established the heavens, I was there,
  when he drew a circle on the face of the deep,
when he made firm the skies above,
  when he established the fountains of the deep,
when he assigned to the sea its limit
  so that the waters might not transgress his command,
when he marked out the foundations of the earth,
  then I was beside him, like a master worker;
and I was daily his delight,
  rejoicing before him always,
rejoicing in his inhabited world
  and delighting in the human race.
PROVERBS 8:24–31

The Genesis account of creation in the Bible is all about order. In fact, the word 'cosmos' literally means 'order'. Yahweh orders the universe. God is not in but above the watery, formless void of the ancient sea; and bit by bit, God puts boundaries on it. God's act of creation is the act of driving chaos back. Land appears when God sets limits on the sea; plants and animals are formed because God tells the sea, 'Here you stop! You may come no further!'

In the beginning when God created the heavens and the earth, the earth was a formless void and darkness covered the face of the deep, while a wind from God swept over the face of the waters. Then God said, 'Let there be light'; and there was light. And God saw that the light was good; and God separated the light from the darkness... And God said, 'Let there be a dome in the midst of the waters, and let it separate the waters from the waters.' So God made the dome and separated the waters that were under the dome from the waters that were above the dome. And it was so. God called the dome Sky... And God said, 'Let the waters under the sky be gathered together in one place, and let the dry land appear.' And it was so. God called the dry land Earth, and the waters that were gathered together he called Seas. And God saw that it was good.
GENESIS 1:1–10

In the imagery of the ancient Jewish scriptures (what Christians call the Old Testament), the primordial sea, and by extension the sea that covers much of the earth's face, is a symbol of all that God is not. The wild, untameable waters at our coastlines are the remnants of the ancient, formless waters that God drove back. That is why they were so frightening to the Israelites. The biblical writers liken them to a fierce dragon, thrashing its scaly tail; a wild, vengeful monster that cannot be calmed. The sea is, in effect, the *un-*creation: it is an undoing; a force of destruction, annihilation and death. It represents everything that leads people away from God, everything that comes between people and the Creator who made and loves them. All through the biblical record, when humans forsake their Creator, order breaks down and chaos comes, quite literally, flooding back in.

That is the warning in the Old Testament story of Noah and the flood. When humans courted evil and violence and began murdering each other, ignoring the poor, abandoning justice and destroying God's precious creation, the waters rose, the deep burst across its boundaries, the heavenly seas crashed through the firmament, and the world lost all of its God-endowed structure. It may be helpful to think of the flood as the seven-day creation story in reverse, like rewinding a film and watching it backwards:

And after seven days the waters of the flood came on the earth. In the six hundredth year of Noah's life, in the second month, on the seventeenth day of the month, on that day all the fountains of the great deep burst forth, and the windows of the heavens were opened. The rain fell on the earth forty days and forty nights... The waters swelled so mightily on the earth that all the high mountains under the whole heaven were covered; the waters swelled above the mountains, covering them fifteen cubits deep. And all flesh died that moved on the earth, birds, domestic animals, wild animals, all swarming creatures that swarm on the earth, and all human beings; everything on dry land in whose nostrils was the breath of life died.
GENESIS 7:10–12, 19–22

According to this account, without God creation is taken apart, piece by piece, until the watery chaos returns.

The story of Jonah and the big fish makes the same point about God. Jonah is the classic curmudgeon who is so angry with God he goes on the run – and all because God told him to deliver a message of rescue to the Assyrians (the arch-enemies of Jonah's people, the Israelites). Jonah cannot abide the idea that God might grant the evil Assyrians mercy, so he flees. Assyria is east of Palestine, so Jonah heads west. At the port of Joppa, he finds a ship preparing to embark on a highly dangerous journey to Tarshish, a mining town then thought to lie on the very western edge of the earth, the edge of solid land, the verge of chaos. So he boards the ship and heads west, with his back to the east, his orient. Thus unable to see his beginnings, his Creator, Jonah heads towards certain destruction.

Now he is at sea, the place he thought to be furthest from the heart and presence of Yahweh. A great storm comes up: the sea monster thrashes its vicious tail; the waters above the firmament split the sky open, thunder roars and lightning strikes terror into Jonah. On board the ship, the sailors fear for their lives. 'Who has caused this storm? Who has angered the gods?' they wonder. It is Jonah. He has made himself Yahweh's enemy by turning to the angry and formless sea for help, rather than to his Maker. The desperate sailors have no choice: they throw him overboard. As Jonah sinks beneath the waves, the storm abates.

There is Jonah in the abyss, drowning – and at this moment he discovers that God loves him as much as God loves the wicked Assyrians. God sends a giant fish to swallow him. For three days, he is in the fish's belly, and then it vomits him out… onto dry land. Never again will Jonah turn to the sea for comfort. Without his Creator, his life plays backwards. The sea dismantles him; in it, his life falls away into uncreated disorder and death.

Early Celtic Christians understood these things about the sea. For them, as for the ancient Jews, the waters of the deep symbolized God's enemies. Living as close as they did to nature, not a day passed when they did not keenly sense the reality of dark, spiritual forces labouring to destroy God's wondrous design. Two places spoke most poignantly to them of the presence of evil: the dark forest, which they dreaded, and the cold, terrifying sea.

3
ISLAND WAYS

Both of the Bible stories of destruction by the sea that we met in chapter two (Noah and the flood, and Jonah and the big fish) begin on land and proceed through a frightening burial in the abyss of the sea. Both stories also finish back on firm earth. They are, in the end, full of hope.

Christians believe that at the moment of humanity's Fall – when humans chose to worship the creation rather than the Creator, thereby destroying the perfect relationship they had enjoyed with God in the Garden of Eden – it was as though the dark, chaotic sea broke through its boundaries and flooded in on humankind, engulfing the entire creation in its meaningless void. Thus doomed in this deep hole of death, people could no longer perceive God, and humanity began its slow and inevitable decay.

And this is precisely the moment that God instigated a new creation plan. This too is described in the stories of Noah and Jonah. We tend to think of these as stories of destruction and death, but in reality they are stories of creation – re-creation to be precise. Think of the ark – the big boat that Noah built to spare himself, his family and pairs of all kinds of animals – being tossed on the violent, seething waves, sinking in the troughs, nearly getting smashed by the breakers swallowing it up. The imagery is that of a tomb. Noah and his family and the representatives of all living things march into it, and the door is shut. Curiously, it is shut not by Noah but by Yahweh, just as a coffin is shut not by the person inside but by the person outside. Noah builds the world's coffin; all of creation is locked inside and the ark is buried in its cold, watery grave.

Fortunately, that is not the end of the story. More than anything, this awful tale of annihilation is ultimately a message of salvation and rescue. For the ark is not only a tomb, it is also a womb. When Noah, his wife and his children, and all the living creatures emerge from the ark, it is as if they are newly born. Clearly, it recounts the original

story of creation that appears in chapter one of Genesis, the first book of the Bible. First, God drives back the overwhelming, disorderly sea and prepares dry land for all of the creatures: 'In the six hundred and first year, in the first month, on the first day of the month, the waters were dried up from the earth; and Noah removed the covering of the ark, and looked, and saw that the face of the ground was drying. In the second month, on the twenty-seventh day of the month, the earth was dry' (Genesis 8:13–14). The same blessing that God had pronounced on the original creation, God then pronounces on this new creation after the flood: 'Be fruitful and multiply on the earth' (Genesis 8:17).

A parallel message appears in the Jonah story. Like the ark, the great fish that swallows Jonah is both a tomb and a womb. Not only is it the dragon from the depths, the monster in whom anarchy and madness dwell, it is also a tiny island that shuts out the wild sea. Inside the fish, Jonah confronts the terrors of death; yet there he is also granted renewed life. What's more, Jonah spends three days in his sea-creature grave, the gestation period before his birth as a new man who will walk in Yahweh's ways. This three-day span is known as the Sign of Jonah, which Christians believe is a sign to the whole world of God's ultimate rescue plan in Jesus. After Jesus' death on a cross, he spent three days in a tomb that also served as a womb, out of which God then raised him to life again, bringing about the birth of a newly made humanity.

What exactly does that mean? Well, it has everything to do with Adam. In the creation account in the book of Genesis, God made Adam, the first human, to dwell as God's close companion in the lush paradise that was the Garden of Eden. Adam (meaning literally 'earth-being') represents our entire species. In its broadest sense, Adam is not the name of one man; it encompasses both Adam and his wife, Eve; it is the name we all share, men and women alike, from every racial and ethnic extraction. Together we are Adam, the earth-people, created from the dust of the ground. Made from humus, the organic matter in soil, we 'humans' have land within our very beings. It was made for us and we belong to it. But this Adam suffers under the curse of death – the result of the fatal error of saying no to God, the source of all life. Separated from God, this Adam, as a species, is fragmented and alone, no longer residing in the paradise called Eden, yet always longing to return to that land, where justice and hope dwell.

The apostle Paul loved to ponder this human dilemma, and he wrote of Jesus as the Second Adam in his first letter to the Corinthians. It was a startling and powerful message of hope. By using this name for Jesus, Paul draws our imaginations back to the Garden of Eden, that glorious, perfect existence. Could it ever be like that again? Yes, Paul tells us. For what humankind, the First Adam, could not do, Jesus in fact did: he conquered death, our most formidable enemy. After three days in the grave, he inexplicably rose to new life. In doing so, he began the re-creation of our species, making possible a new Adam, a newly created humanity, for whom death is not the final word – a new Adam walking towards a new Eden. How was Jesus able to accomplish such a colossal task? Because of who he was: God incarnate, God in flesh. Christians believe that Jesus was simultaneously fully human and fully God. In a mystery that finite human minds can never completely grasp, God visited our planet in the form of a man and lived among us. In Jesus, he shared our human nature. Jesus, the God-man, revealed what human life was meant to be: full and complete friendship with the Creator. In Jesus, the human race finally and fully said yes to God. Jesus demonstrated that true life comes only from God, and that this life is not about greed and injustice and human pride, but about love, humility and selflessness. In Jesus, God poured self-sacrificing love on this broken and lonely world. Death, the natural penalty of forsaking the God of life, could not hold Jesus, because as a man, he perfectly said yes to God in every fibre of his being. Through Jesus,

God is working to reunite everything in the world that is fractured and out of joint.

With a passion that is total and infinite, God plans and promises the redemption of the entire creation. Immediately after the sea figuratively crosses its boundaries after the Fall of Adam and Eve in Eden, God once again sets limits for it. Over and over, humans keep inviting the sea back in, and over and over, God keeps driving it back. One day, the plan will be completed and Eden will be fully restored. When that day dawns, not only will the sea of death and disorder never again cross its boundaries, it will also cease to exist. This is the vision that the Gospel-writer John, as an old man, saw in his revelation on the island of Patmos. Like Paul, John too had pondered the heart-wrenching plight of human existence. He was one of Jesus' original followers and closest friends. As an eyewitness to Jesus' death on the cross and a believer in his doom-shattering resurrection, he was utterly convinced that Jesus was indeed the Second Adam, the hope of humanity. John's brilliantly symbolic and poetic apocalyptic vision is recorded in Revelation, the Bible's final book. The concluding part of his vision starts like this: 'Then I saw a new heaven and a new earth; for the first heaven and the first earth had passed away, and the sea was no more' (Revelation 21:1).

But what should people do in the meantime? While awaiting God's final rescue of the world, how do humans survive the ongoing battle against the sea of fear and uncertainty, the storms of violence and injustice, the turbulent waters of sickness and suffering, and the waves of defeat and hopelessness that engulf every human life? Survival is possible through commitment to island ways. Christians believe that God has broken through the noise and confusion of our troubled world. No matter how overwhelmingly the waters rise and seethe, God provides solid and secure islands of peace and order – islands of the Spirit's presence. These are places to experience God's overwhelming goodness, guidance and strength. In the glory of the created world, and in the still, small whisper of God's voice deep within, theophanies, or 'God-showings', occur without number. The Celtic Christians had a special term for these experiences: they called them 'thin places', places where the veil between this world of disorder and death and the world of God's reign is so thin, one can all but step through it.

Many people have experienced glorious encounters with nature, when for just a moment they caught a glimpse of a renewed Eden. Sometimes people have this experience while hiking in the mountains, or witnessing a spectacular sunset. Sometimes a person steps outside on a winter's day and is suddenly struck by the unspeakable beauty of bare tree branches against a cold, grey sky. These are moments when creation itself is shouting of the glory of the Creator, and when it is possible to encounter Yahweh's immense love and grace in a very personal way.

Celtic Christians today have come to associate this idea of thin places with regions of great natural beauty, and some of these places are known as sacred spaces. They are called this because they are places where an encounter with God has had significance not just for its immediate receiver, but for an entire nation – or indeed for all people everywhere. Mount Sinai, where, according to the Bible, Moses directly encountered God and received two tablets with the ten commandments inscribed on them, is an example of a sacred space. But the miraculous event that occurred there was not meant just for Moses – it was for the entire world. For humanity, Mount Sinai is a sacred space, a set-apart space, because God, in effect, spoke to all people there; it was a theophany for humankind. It is possible, however, to make the mistake of thinking there is something magical about Mount Sinai. It may be tempting to believe that the mountain is sacred in and of itself. This is not to say that the mountain is devoid of meaning, and even glory. It is full of meaning because it is part of God's creation, and God was revealed

through it. What makes it especially set apart, though, is that the sacred God came *to* it.

This idea that God meets with people through the material world was passionately embraced by the early Celtic Christians. It is what Christians call the doctrine of incarnation: God creates matter and is then revealed to people in and through it. Ultimately, God entered the world in the body of a helpless infant – Jesus. God's disclosure to humanity is all about incarnation – God taking on flesh – and it can only occur in one direction: us-ward. Try as one might, it is impossible to climb to God; God comes down to us. And that is exactly why any place in the universe can be a thin place. It was, after all, in the belly of a slimy fish that Jonah encountered God, and not because there was anything especially sacred about that fish's inner chambers. What made the fish such a sacred space is who came *to* it: God.

Becoming open to island ways – that is, living in wait for God's new creation to break in and waiting for its promised completion – means opening the heart to some very unexpected thin places. This is not to say that Christians go around merely looking for the 'magic' of a particular place, although it is true that certain places exist that are, by their own nature, very special, where God's presence may be sensed more powerfully than elsewhere. Often this is because the sheer beauty of the place declares the glory of God; and often it is because of a long tradition of prayer in a particular place. The special sanctity of these locations is real and extremely important, but in general it is not necessary to go in search of sacred places. Instead, it is better to spend life's journey asking God to draw near, and being genuinely surprised at where those encounters with God occur. This is because the thinnest place in one's life might actually be, metaphorically speaking, on the sea – the place that appears to be furthest from God's goodness – or in a storm. When Moses encountered God on Mount Sinai, it was within an ominous-looking cloud that blotted out the sun. The biblical account states that 'Moses drew near to the thick darkness where God was'. Yahweh loves to bring light into people's darkness and order into their confusion. That is what God did in the act of creation, and that is what God is still about – re-creating and renewing Eden, putting boundaries on the sea, even in the smallest concerns of daily life.

In the following three chapters, we will consider three Celtic isles, which are holy, or set apart, because of what occurred on them. All three islands are places where, ages ago, some very intrepid people decided to seek God no matter what the cost. They turned their backs to an ocean of worldly temptations – wealth, status, political power – and planted themselves on these islands of God's goodness. And God met them. Here their lives of dedicated prayer and service to others were played out. Here are the places where they laboured for years to copy the holy scriptures; where they rose several times a night from their plain beds of earth and straw to make intercessory prayer for the sick and lonely who visited their monasteries; where they gathered together daily to chant the Psalms, all 150 of them every week, from memory.

These islands are thin places, where God heard the heart cries of simple monks and nuns and answered. Still today, from these tiny slabs of firm earth, the chaos monster retreats. They are models for people seeking to hear God's voice despite the noise of their demanding modern lives threatening to drown it out, and despite all of the forces that suck them under and tow them out to the crushing, suffocating void. It is on islands such as these that people must perpetually dwell, or face life without God. We may visit them in person, or vicariously through this book; but however we acquaint ourselves with their geography, we should try at all costs to make it the geography of our souls. By adopting the island ways of God's Spirit, despite being surrounded on all sides by the dragon of the deep, it is possible to live as part of God's new creation, rooted in its peace and security, making it the only habitation, and furthering its spread.

Each of our three islands has its own personality, its own way of confronting the dread sea serpent. Aran, off the west coast of Ireland, is a bare and rocky landscape, exposed to the full force of brutal Atlantic storms. And yet its name means 'the inhabited place'. Confronting the fiercest gales, it declares itself Land. The tiny Isle of Iona, off Scotland's west coast, is famous for being the sunniest place in all of Scotland. It is a long journey to Iona from the mainland, requiring first a trip across the substantial Isle of Mull, but the tranquillity on this all-but-car-free slice of soil and rock is unparalleled. The opposite of Aran, it is Calm itself, and offers a taste of the peace of the future new creation, the Garden of Eden restored. Finally the Holy Island of Lindisfarne, off the north-east coast of England, is our tidal island. Twice a day, when the tide goes out, a person can cross unharmed from the island to the mainland, and back again. It tells of the ebb and flow of life with God in a yet-to-be-transformed world: it is the tension between the here-and-now reality of God's Spirit dwelling within people – for God takes up residence deep within our beings as we say yes to God's offer of love and forgiveness – and the not-yet of the final redemption of the entire creation. Lindisfarne gives a taste of the end of Sea, when a person can cross safely, without fear. At the same time, it speaks of the necessity of leaving the secure island to minister to a world suffering from the harsh realities of a mainland swamped by storms – the primordial sea violating its boundaries. It is from Lindisfarne that a person ventures to work in the world, and it is to the safety of Lindisfarne that one must return before the tide rolls back in.

And so we begin our island hopping.

II
ISLANDS

4

STORM OF ARAN

Aran, also known as Inis Mor, is the largest of the three tiny Aran Islands off Ireland's west coast. Eight-and-a-half miles long and two miles wide (13.7 kilometres by 3.2 kilometres), aligned north-west to south-east, Aran is a defiant habitation. No one should be able to live here; yet it has supported generations of families for thousands of years.

Through the millennia, its barren, wind-battered, grey limestone has been subject every moment to the violent impulses of the Atlantic. It was here, early in the sixth century AD that St Enda established his monastery. Perhaps he was drawn to the immense silence of the place, perfect for a contemplative life; to the dense swirling fogs that envelop the eastern coastline for half the year, obliterating the often-tempting views of the mainland; and to the ruggedness of stones and storms. It was perfect for Enda's monastic ambitions: to devote himself to prayer and contemplation, and to face the hardships of a life stripped of luxury. On Aran he would learn what it meant to confront the

Aran

barrenness of earthly existence while living in expectation of the promised future Eden.

He already knew something of hardship and the reality of death. The son of a king, Prince Enda was a trained warrior who fought in some brutal battles. His sister Fanchea, who was a nun, pleaded with him to forsake his life of blood and war and was, in the end, so persuasive that Enda left the military with plans to marry a young postulate at Fanchea's monastery. On the same day that the girl accepted his proposal (not that she had any choice: Prince Enda had the right to demand her acceptance), she died. When Enda viewed her body, the reality of the shortness of life struck him so deeply that he vowed to live the rest of his own in seeking and serving God. And so he eventually journeyed to this bare and storm-afflicted island.

On Aran's western and southern bounds stand sheer, high cliff faces, which take the full force of ocean onslaughts that speed and swell from across the entire Atlantic. By the time these mountains of water reach the island, they are powerful enough to shear off great chunks of rock from the cliffs that dare to stop them, hurling the huge stones back at a cliff's face – and even over the top. These massive, sheared-off boulders form lines of 'storm beaches'.

Further inland from the Atlantic, the vertical cliffs give way to the slanting planes of grey limestone that cover most of the island. Deep fissures cross-hatch the stone, through which precious rain water flows and disappears. Finally, on the gentler northern and eastern sides of the island, the limestone tables give way to expansive sand beaches, dunes and drifts.

Two things immediately strike the visitor. Firstly, the silence. Secondly, the thousands of miles of drystone fences marching in close order over the entire island, dividing it into an intricate network of tiny gardens and pastures, most just large enough for one or two cows. Large parts of the island have no indigenous soil. But generations of islanders in defiance of the erosive winds actually manufactured soil through the agonizing work of hauling lime-rich sand from the beaches up to the rock tables. They bent their backs filling the deep cracks in the limestone with smaller rocks, then they spread the precious sand on top of the grey stone, adding seaweed for fertilizer.

What St Enda found is that, even on this island of stone, so frequently subjected to the fiercest of storms, life thrives and creates awe-inspiring beauty. The pilgrim today discovers a world of strange sounds punctuating the stillness – the rush of the sea spouting through inland puffing holes, the wind chanting eerily as it whips through the drystone walls, the screaming of the cliff-nesting birds. There is a visual feast too – the prints of shore birds' tiny feet in the sand; weird pockmarks everywhere, like alien footsteps in limestone; the stunning contrast between vast, blue sky and flat, grey rock; and endless arrays of ferns and delicate flowers growing from the stone's deep fissures.

So many monks and nuns came to study at Enda's monastery that he gained a lofty reputation as the father of Irish monasticism. Some of his students remained on the island, setting up monasteries of their own. The landscape is littered with the remains of ancient churches and beehive cells, where hundreds of medieval monks worshipped, prayed, transcribed books, gardened, fished, ate and slept in tranquillity. Others left this wild place for the mainland, to establish monasteries of their own and to spread Christianity throughout Ireland and beyond. What they learned about enduring the storms on Aran got them through storms of a different nature in the landscapes of their later lives.

Ocean Blessing

God the Father, all-powerful, benign,
Jesu, the Son of tears and of sorrow,
With thy co-assistance, O Holy Spirit!

The Three-One, ever-living, ever-mighty, everlasting,
Who brought the Children of Israel through the Red Sea,
And Jonah to land from the belly of the great creature of
   the ocean,

Who brought Paul and his companions in the ship,
From the torment of the sea, from the sorrow of the waves,
From the great gale, from the heavy storm,

Protect us and shield and sanctify us,
Be seated, O King of the elements, at our helm,
And lead us in peace to the end of our journey.

ADAPTED FROM *CARMINA GADELICA*

Storm

Far on the Atlantic, waves rise
Like mountains on the sea.
Soon come their warrior cries.

God out-shouts them,
Thunders from the skies.
God's voice majestic
Shakes the coast,
Roars and commands in
Lightning bolts,
Flattens oaks,
Lays the old woodland bare.

While angels' tongues sing
'Glory! Glory!'
God reigns above the flood on air,
Holds out the sceptre,
Orders the waves to cease.

God grants the people
Strength, and peace.

BASED ON PSALM 29

THE LIQUID SHORE

Along the liquid shore
No boundary clearly forms
Between the sea and land
But what comes in the storms.

For then the dance is done,
The gliding 'cross the floor;
The sea intrudes and begs,
But land declares, 'No more.'

St Benan's Church

There are times
When the sea rolls in with force.
It comes in vicious, swamping waves that
Choke our breath and drown our hopes.
Mountains of moving water they are,
That hurl their entire selves onto our
Shores and then have the audacity to send
Liquid fingers, like crab legs, slithering
Across our beaches and over our boundary rocks.

There is no winning with the sea.
Its power is complete, its killing cold is
Too deep to be warmed,
Even by the white-hot sun.
A person cannot battle the sea.

But there is the stopping of it.
For solid rock
Burst from the ocean's
Depths. It came erupting, quaking and
Exploding with molten heat that the
Sea could not quench.

It spewed fire in grand defiance of its
Formless, watery bed.
Then this burning lava froze,
Locked its molecules in place. Refused
To budge. Massive, solid, unmoving,
It said to the sea, 'Here you stop!

You cannot climb me!
I am Land.'

On the very top of Aran's hills
Is a tiny oratory – a stone chapel,
The Church of St Benan –
Just big enough for a grown person
With arms outstretched
To touch the walls on either side.
Thick stone ramparts make a fortress for one,
A hideaway at the top of the world.

Up there you cannot even hear the sea,
Only the wind, which blows like God's
Spirit: unpredictable and strong.

The climb to the church is steep,
But not rough.
Looking from its little
Window, the view is of high and hilly
Land, lots of land, lots and lots of
Solid, unmoving rock.
Rock that is so high, so full of
Shape and form, and so changeless,
The sea shrinks from it.

This is where we go when the sea comes in.
We go up the steep hill to our little oratory,
To the land and the sky and the wind.
The stone walls enfold us and we can, at last,
Hear God's voice.

Stone Memorials

Lining the coastal road that
Encircles Aran are stone memorials
To fisher folk lost at sea. Many young
Men never returned home because the
Sea claimed them.

Sorrow is what swells the sea.
Yet even this cold, deep graveyard
Yields good things: fish,
Crustaceans,
Mammals, even;
Shells,
Seaweed (for food and soil),
Beauty,
Rhythm.
And this formless
Liquid somehow supports solid currachs,
Small, hide-covered basket boats,
With fishermen in them who ride atop the
Waves unharmed and claim the sea's bounty.

PRAYER OF THE CELTIC FISHERMAN

O God, the sea is so great
And my boat is so small.

TRADITIONAL

Thou, My Soul's Healer

Thou, my soul's Healer,
Keep me at even,
Keep me at morning,
Keep me at noon,
On rough course faring,
Help and safeguard
My means this night.
I am tired, astray, and stumbling,
Shield Thou me from snare and sin.

Carmina Gadelica

Boundary Sands

I placed the sand as a boundary for the sea,
  a perpetual barrier that it cannot pass;
though the waves toss, they cannot prevail,
    though they roar, they cannot pass over it.

Jeremiah 5:22

BUN GABHLA

Here is the coast of Bun Gabhla
At Aran's western tip,
Lonely, lovely beachhead
For launching currachs.

It is a moonscape of
Massive boulders,
Some as huge as
Small dwellings,

Solid rooms through which
Sea water cannot flow;
Rooms without doors.

The sea – this is a battle strategy –
Flung them onto the shore,
Where they remain unmoved in
Heaps, like silent, storeyed fortresses.

This deadly arsenal,
Discharged in wrath at Aran,
Was not (truth be told) about war.
It was all because it refused digestion.
This fact is what sent the grey swells into battle.
It infuriated the sea to discover that,
Even in its own depths,
Land existed.

GRASS AND SOIL

How do grasses grow
In this thin soil?
How does soil settle
On this bare rock?

It settles,
Layer by layer,
Due to love-labour.
It was a love of
Island ways that
Led generations of hands
To tuck the seaweed into
Rock crevices,
Year after year.

Love makes its own soil
Where soil is not.
Life-giving grains,
Even flowers,
Spring out of rock.

LIKE A MOTHER EAGLE

Like a mother eagle who gathers
Her young under her wings,
God is our storm shelter.

Like helpless chicks with
No flight in us, we run to
Her soft, dry hiding place.

The winds buffet her body,
But beneath her feathers
We sit unmoved.

We take her warmth and
Her strength;
She is our sun and rock,

Until the storm is past
And we can try our wings
Again.

THE STORM OF HOPELESSNESS

In the hopelessness of poverty,
God of the poor,
Aid me.

In the crush of defeat,
God of the downtrodden,
Lift me.

In the despair of loneliness,
God of the forsaken,
Comfort me.

In the grip of guilt,
God of the defenceless,
Free me.

In the anxiety of life,
God of the troubled,
Calm me and grant me your peace.

Earth and Wind

It is he who made the earth by his power,
  who established the world by his wisdom,
  and by his understanding stretched out the heavens.
When he utters his voice, there is a tumult of waters in the
  heavens,
  and he makes the mist rise from the ends of the earth.
He makes lightnings for the rain,
  and he brings out the wind from his storehouses.

Jeremiah 10:12–13

THE DESIRED HAVEN

Some went down to the sea in ships,
   doing business on the mighty waters;
they saw the deeds of the Lord,
   his wondrous works in the deep.
For he commanded and raised the stormy wind,
   which lifted up the waves of the sea.
They mounted up to heaven, they went down to the depths;
   their courage melted away in their calamity;
they reeled and staggered like drunkards,
   and were at their wits' end.

Then they cried to the Lord in their trouble,
   and he brought them out from their distress;
he made the storm be still,
   and the waves of the sea were hushed.
Then they were glad because they had quiet,
   and he brought them to their desired haven.
Let them thank the Lord for his steadfast love,
   for his wonderful works to humankind.
Let them extol him in the congregation of the people,
   and praise him in the assembly of the elders.

PSALM 107:23–32

A Prayer of Protection

O God who pervades the heights,
Imprint on us your gracious blessing,
Carry us over the surface of the sea,
Carry us safely to a haven of peace,
Bless our boatmen and our boat,
Bless our anchors and our oars,
Each stay and halyard and traveller.
From our mainsails to our tall masts –
Keep them, O King of the elements, in their
    place,
That we may return home in peace.

Pour down from above the dew
That makes our faith grow,
Establish us in the Rock of rocks,
In every law that love exhibits,
That we may reach the land of glory,
Where peace and love and mercy reign,
Bestowed on us through grace.

Cast the serpent into the ocean,
So that the sea may swallow it up;
Reveal the storm from the north,
Quell its wrath and blunt its fury,
Lessen its fierceness, kill its cold.

Subdue the crest of the waves,
Ward off the storm from the west;
Each day and night, storm and calm,
Be with us, O Chief of chiefs,
Be our compass-chart,
Be the hand on the helm of our rudder,
Your own hand, O God of the elements,
Early and late, each day and night.

Amen.

ADAPTED FROM *CARMINA GADELICA*

5
CALM OF IONA

There is reason to believe that St Columba, when he was a very young man living in Ireland, visited St Enda's monastery on Aran – as did a great number of other Irish saints, abbots and abbesses. The young Columba shared common ground with the aged Enda: they were both Irish-born and of royal lineage, both princes of their respective tribes and had both been trained as warriors. Enda, of course, had long since renounced his life as a man of war, but Columba was still young and fiery by nature. No doubt Enda and his monks tried their best to rid Columba of his fierce instincts for battle. It did not work, however. Upon leaving Aran, some believe he battled within his own soul a storm that took years to abate; he lived with the constant tension between his powerful devotion to Christ and his warrior's temperament.

For years, he channelled his passions into establishing thriving and influential monasteries all over Ireland, promoting the same godly devotion and radical love of the poor as Enda. Then, in the year 563, at the age of 42, his unquenchable energy and fiery spirit exploded in an event that carried him from his beloved Ireland to establish a new monastic settlement on the tiny Isle of Iona off the west coast of Scotland. The stories say that he left Ireland because he broke his priestly vows by raising an army to fight the high king – who had wrested the kingship from Columba's tribe, the Ui Neill. Columba also had a personal grudge against the king, a grudge he had allowed to simmer for decades. When Columba was a much younger man, the king had ruled against him in a dispute between Columba and the abbot under whom he was studying. At long last, Columba had found an excuse to go to war against the king. He called up an army from his own tribe and won – but at a huge cost. Hundreds of young men and women fell in the battle. As penance, Columba left Ireland to win as many souls to Christ as he had just seen killed. He went to Iona to begin again, and here he finally and completely turned his back on the storms of violence and war and devoted the rest of his life to the peace that comes only from God's Spirit. And peace is still a palpable presence on this tiny island.

Iona, which means 'beautiful island', is a taste of the new Eden yet to come. Columba was true to his commitment: here he spent long hours in prayerful solitude; he communed with angels; he ordered all weapons on the island to be destroyed; through prayer and fasting, he drove back armies of demons that sought to harm his monks; and in the name of Christ, he calmed storms at sea and commanded a sea serpent to be gone. As much as Columba had given himself over to battle as a young man, he now laboured even more to teach and demonstrate God's infinite love for creation. He gained a reputation as Columba the Benign, and his great tenderness towards both people and animals affected all who met him. Iona is indeed a 'thin place', with a 1,500-year tradition of prayer, by which evil has been driven out and God's peace instilled.

Iona

Columba chose Iona as both his true home and what he called his 'place of resurrection' – meaning the place where he would die and from which he would be raised to new life in the restored creation. He died on 9 June 597 at the age of 75. Just before his death, his last words to his monks were, 'Let everyone live together in peace.'

On Iona, the peace of a final and complete refuge from the storm is keenly felt. It provides a foretaste of the perfectly restored creation to come, a place where war will cease and lions will lie down with lambs. The peace of Iona is far more than a temporary retreat – it gives people the courage and the faith to continue their journey through the troubled here-and-now, knowing that we travel towards a better country, whose founder and ruler is God.

COLMCILLE

On some island I long to be,
a rocky promontory, looking on
the coiling surface of the sea.

To see the waves, crest on crest
of the great shining ocean, composing
a hymn to the creator, without rest.

To see without sadness the strand
lined with bright shells, and birds
lamenting overhead, a lonely sound.

To hear the whisper of small waves
against the rocks, that endless sea-
sound, like keening over graves.

To watch the sea-birds sailing
in flocks, and most marvellous
of monsters, the turning whale.

To see the shift from ebb tide
to flood and tell my secret name:
'He who set his back on Ireland.'

JOHN MONTAGUE

Note: Colmcille is Columba's Irish name, meaning 'Dove of the Church'

Aurora

When Autumn's chill had chased away the sun,
And days were short and long nights had begun,
The dark's broad cloak descended on this isle.
We settled and prepared for Winter's trial.

Three nights I ventured to the rocky shore,
While stars lay sprinkled on the heavens' floor.
The moon was blotted out, my path obscured,
Yet, calm before the waves, the coast endured.

Then 'cross the Sound of Mull strange blazes shone
And shot above the hills, cone upon cone.
While hard below, deep blackness held its sway,
Bright dancing lights above the earth played day.

As if a host of angels sallied forth,
Aurora's shim'ring arms still pointed north.

GOD'S ANGELS

May God's angels protect me,
Hold me up –
Strong hands beneath
My elbows –
On stony path,
On cliff's edge,
In darkest forest,
In deepest pit.

May God's angels comfort me
With the comfort of God's arms.
May God's angels lead me
With the strength of God's hands.
For every day they dwell in God's
    presence.
God is who they know.

Amen.

HERMIT'S CELL

(A FORMULA FOR PRAYER)

In secret cell,
Alone with God,
On adoration first I dwell.

In secret cell,
Alone with God,
Of all my faults and fears I tell.

In secret cell,
Alone with God,
Thanksgivings start to rise and swell.

In secret cell,
Alone with God,
Appeals are my monastic bell.

And God says,
'Fear not,
All is well.'

NIGHT PRAYER

Shield me, O God, this night,
From all the powers that hurt,
As I lie down in silence
Between the earth and the heavens.

Wrap me, O God, this night,
In the warm cloak of your love,
As I lie down in silence
Between my floor and my roof.

Hold me, O God, this night,
In your tender embrace,
As I lie down in silence
Between all below and all above,

As I lie down in silence,
Cradled in your arms,
Beneath me, around me, rocking me
Between the earth and the heavens.

NO WEAPONS

Let there be no
Weapons of war
In my home.

Let there be no
Instruments
That wound.

No sarcasm,
No biting words,
No bitterness, or wrath,
No strife, or judgment,
No simmering resentment.

Each weapon broken;
Each wound healed;
Each mind and heart
Renewed by the
Compassion and
Forgiveness of God.

Amen.

STONE CROSSES

Everywhere I go on Iona
I encounter stone crosses.
Each stands between me and the sea,
Between me and chaos, between me and fear,
Between me and the power of the deep,
Between me and death.

Like silent sentinels they mark the
Boundary between this world of stone and
Soil and the unseen world.

How can I enter that other world
Where life is more solid even than
These stones? The cross is the door in,
The threshold on which God killed
Death and invited humanity into a
New land. The crosses on Iona tell
This story. I read the pictures
Carved all over their faces, that
Recount the ancient saga of our plight,
And the grand, earth-shattering
Scheme of redemption.

They tower above me, these stone pillars,
With the authority of the Creator. Up, up,
Up, my eyes travel, from the solid, square
Shaft, to the cross beam, to the great,
Encompassing circle of love, forever
Locking the outstretched arms to the
Body. Then to the very top, where there is
Only bright blue sky, clear quiet air.

For a moment, I'm lifted to those heights.
Then as Celtic Christians once did, I fall
To the ground, prostrating myself
Before the greatest wonder in the
Universe – everywhere I go.

THE BRAVE SUN

Each night the brave sun
Lies down in the sea, without fear.

As the black waves bury him,
He flings over his head a comforter of crimson glory,
Pulls it tight and slumbers safely in the depths.

Each morning he rises,
Shakes off his red-orange bedclothes and
Marches on the waves like a king,
Unwounded and triumphant.

PILGRIMAGE

Those who find their strength in you,
O Three of Life,
Are blessed.

Those whose life is a pilgrimage to your land,
O Three of Heaven,
Are blessed.

For when their path descends through Weeping Valley
    in Autumn,
Their tears awaken hidden springs.

Late rains make
Pools of water,
Everywhere.

Within their souls,
Fountains bubble,
Fountains of strength upon strength.

Then Weeping Valley Road ascends,
Turns sharply right and ends
At heaven's gate.

BASED ON PSALM 84:5–7

LEVIATHAN CRUSHED

Yet God my King is from of old,
working salvation in the earth.
You divided the sea by your might;
you broke the heads of the dragons in the waters.
You crushed the heads of Leviathan;
you gave him as food for the creatures of the
wilderness.
You cut openings for springs and torrents;
you dried up ever-flowing streams.
Yours is the day, yours also the night;
you established the luminaries and the sun.
You have fixed all the bounds of the earth;
you made summer and winter.

PSALM 74:12–17

RULER OF THE ELEMENTS

Who is on the tiller of my rudder,
Giving speed to my east-bound barge?
Peter and Paul and John the Baptist are all there.
Christ sits on my helm, guiding my boat through the winds.

For whom does the voice of the wind tremble?
For whom do the waves of the strait become quiet?
For Jesus Christ, Chief of each saint,
The Son of Mary,
The Root of Victory.

CARMINA GADELICA

Columba's Bay

Here I turn my back:
On past regrets,
On fear,
On the chaos of the sea,
On all anxieties that
Keep me from God.

Here I turn my back:
On anger,
On rage,
On arrogance,
On the pride that
Stands between me and God.

Here I turn my back:
On cynicism,
On contempt,
On scorn,
On all dark doubts that
Destroy my faith in God.

Here I turn my face,
My heart,
My body,
My whole being
To you, O God.
To you, O God of life and love.

Amen.

God of Three Faces

God of Three Faces,
Grant me your strength,
Grant me your will,
Grant me your peace.

The strength of the Father,
Who hovered over chaos and tamed it.

The will of the Son,
Who walked upon the angry waves.

The peace of the Spirit,
Who wells up like springs in my dry soul.

A Peace Blessing

Peace of the ebbing tide to you,
Peace of the firmest ground to you,
Peace of the gently setting sun to you,
Peace of the smiling, rising moon to you,
Peace of the night sky to you,
Peace of the morning's hope to you.
The peace of all peace be to you,
This day, this night, and evermore.

Amen.

6

EBB AND FLOW OF LINDISFARNE

Columba spent more than 30 years on his beloved Iona, but in truth, he was not always on the island. Iona was the pier from which he launched his multiple and tenacious missionary efforts among the Picts of northern Scotland. He fought Brude, king of the Picts, not by conventional warfare but with his new and far more powerful arsenal of weapons: prayer, fasting and love. It was desperately hard work, and sometimes Columba despaired of ever reaching this tribe with the news of God's infinite love.

But he never gave up, and his efforts eventually resulted in the spread of the Christian faith across Scotland.

Columba's students followed suit. Faithful to his example, generations of Iona monks left the calm of their lovely isle and devoted – and often risked – their lives to minister to a suffering world. They expanded Columba's missionary vision, carrying the light of Christ's freedom and love to northern England and throughout Europe.

St Aidan was one of these devoted monks. Like Columba,

Lindisfarne

he too was from Ireland, but for many years he had lived among
the monastic community on Iona. Oswald, the young prince of
Northumbria, land of the Angles, in what is now northern England,
had also lived on Iona. He was not a monk, however; he was living
in exile until he could gain his kingdom from Edwin, his uncle.
When at last that day came, he returned to Northumbria and began
his benevolent rule. Seventeen years on Iona had meant that he had
been schooled in the Christian faith, and now he wanted to share
with his subjects what he knew of Christian charity. He sent word
to the brothers on Iona: 'Please send a missionary to minister to the
Anglian people.' The monks knew that Aidan was perfect for the
job. Newly ordained as a bishop, he took a group of Iona monks with
him, and Oswald granted them the tiny island of Lindisfarne, off the

north-east coast of England, for their monastic home.

Northumbria was torn by the conflict between the Celts and the Angles. The inhabitants were hardened by years of fighting; a heavy hand would only cause them to rebel. It was Aidan's profound gentleness, the true gentleness of Jesus, that won them over. His unusual spirit of sacrifice and generosity towards the poor amazed both Oswald and his people.

Iona's peace travelled with Aidan to his new country. For days and weeks throughout the year, and always for the forty days of Lent, he retreated to Inner Farne, an even smaller island beyond Lindisfarne. Inner Farne was his Iona – his refuge and place of solitude and prayer. His time on Inner Farne bestowed on him the fortitude to go on long, arduous journeys all over Northumbria. Aidan's life took on a rhythm typical of many Celtic monks: retreat and service, retreat and service. In Aidan's new monastery, this rhythm was mirrored by the rhythm of the tides, for Lindisfarne is not an island in the true sense of the word. Twice a day, when the tide goes out, it is connected to the mainland. Today, a person can travel safely to and from the island either by walking across the three miles of tidal flats, as Aidan would have done, or driving across the raised causeway that appears as the water retreats.

When the tide went out, Aidan would frequently leave the serenity of Lindisfarne and venture into the troubled world of Northumbria. He was famous for walking mile upon mile, for weeks and even months at a time, visiting the sick, aiding the poor and teaching everyone he met about Jesus, the Saviour of the world. King Oswald was so appreciative, he gave Aidan a prize horse to carry him on his long journeys. No sooner did Aidan leave with his new mount, than a poor beggar on the road asked him for alms. Without a thought, Aidan gave him the horse! The beggar, he later explained to Oswald, was of even greater value than the animal.

The Holy Island of Lindisfarne is, metaphorically, where many people live the greater part of their lives. As they seek to follow God, they are sometimes called to endure violent storms, like those on Aran. And there are times when they are granted the healing peace and vision of hope of the lovely Iona. But day to day, it is Lindisfarne that defines their lives. Everyone has a quiet place, deep within their souls, where God meets them and fills them and teaches them. In the safety of this place, it is possible to gain the resolve to cross the causeway and minister to a hurting world. One's life can achieve the rhythm of Aidan's: solitude, then service; solitude, then service. But the rhythm must be maintained. Lingering too long on the mainland, without regular retreat to island time with God, allows weakness and fear to creep in. However, remaining only on the island, never noticing that the tide has gone out and that God is beckoning from the mainland, means Jesus' work of suffering with a world that longs to know God stays undone.

The tidal island is where we live between Aran and Iona, between the storm and God's perfect kingdom. In the ebb and flow of life, weeping with the grief-stricken, comforting the dying, tending the sick, feeding the hungry, rejoicing with the rescued and simply giving a cup of cold water to someone in Jesus' name, Aidan is a reminder that Jesus is ever-present throughout the journey across the tidal flats in retreat and service, retreat and service.

AIDAN'S PRAYER

Blest tiny and beloved isle,
Where solitude and goodness dwell,
My refuge from a thousand ills
Of wind and surf and angry swell,

Be now an island in my heart
That when I travel from this place,
By rich imagination's spell,
You'll go with me and keep apace.

Upon your solid rocks I'll walk,
Your bound'ries ev'ry wave shall quell;
The fear that tightens its embrace
Shall flee when tolls your hourly bell.

So my poor heart shall dwell in peace,
Though through the storm my boat must race,
Your presence, my monastic cell
Of strength and confidence and grace.

MY ISLAND

God of ledge and cave,
You are my shelter
In the biting wind.

God of sturdy branch,
You are my pilgrim's staff
For the steep and lonely road.

God of streaming light,
You are my eyes
In my blindness.

God of solid earth,
You are my island
When I'm lost at sea.

My Pilgrim's Staff

I leave my island
Of rest,
Of solitude,
Of peace,
Of security.

I cross the tidal flats
To work,
To weariness,
To fear,
To uncertainty.

I carry my pilgrim's staff
Of steadiness,
Of hope,
Of companionship,
Of surety:

The steadiness of the Spirit's presence,
The hope of Christ's defeat of death,
The companionship of the Great Three,
The surety of God's eternal love.

WALKING WITH GOD

If God does not march before me,
The sea will not part.

If God does not walk beside me,
The path will not reveal itself.

If God does not rule above me,
The rain will pelt without mercy.

If God does not follow behind me,
The tide will take me unawares.

If the Three of Life dwells within me,
My soul and my body will rise to life eternal.

THE WINDS

But God remembered Noah and all the wild animals and all the domestic animals that were with him in the ark. And God made a wind blow over the earth, and the waters subsided; the fountains of the deep and the windows of the heavens were closed, the rain from the heavens was restrained, and the waters gradually receded from the earth.

GENESIS 8:1–3

Then Moses stretched out his hand over the sea. The Lord drove the sea back by a strong east wind all night, and turned the sea into dry land; and the waters were divided. The Israelites went into the sea on dry ground, the waters forming a wall for them on their right and on their left.

EXODUS 14:21–22

HOLDING THE CHRIST-LIGHT

There is a candle,
Solitaire,
Thought spare
By showy candle ware:
No sun-like heat,
No dawn-like glow,
No strobe,
No flare,
No row on row.

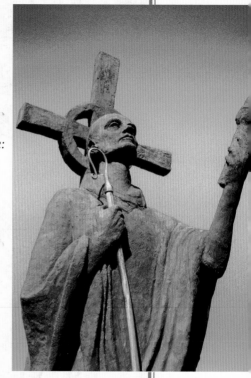

It stands alone
So straight and tall
It sometimes seems
Not there at all;
Yet on a steep and lightless trail
Its beam shines bright and does not fail.

Through biting wind,
In pelting rain,
Its wick, undaunted,
Burns the same.
Where feet may slip on coarser stuff,
It gives its light.
It is enough.

AIDAN'S PATH

Each day may I walk the path that
Aidan walked:
To the poor,
To the sick,
To the lonely.

Each day may I deliver the compassionate
Love of Jesu:
To the poor,
To the sick,
To the lonely.

Each night may I return to Holy Island
Where Aidan prayed:
For the poor,
For the sick,
For the lonely,

Where Aidan prayed to the One
Who always
Helps the poor,
Heals the sick,
Harbours the lonely.

THANKSGIVING

Thanks be to Thee, O God, that I have risen today,
To the rising of this life itself;
May it be to Thine own glory, O God of every gift,
And to the glory of my soul likewise.

O great God, aid Thou my soul
With the aiding of Thine own mercy;
Even as I clothe my body with wool,
Cover Thou my soul with the shadow of Thy wing.

Help me to avoid every sin,
And the source of sin to forsake;
And as the mist scatters on the crest of the hills,
May each ill haze clear from my soul, O God.

CARMINA GADELICA

DWELLING ON HOLY ISLAND

There are days when I feel I cannot cross the
Channel to the world of busyness and work and
Human relationships.

The tide of care rolls in and I have neither a boat
Nor the strength to cross. It is too daunting,
Too frightening, too cold and bitter, too dangerous.

On those days I need to dwell on the
Holy Island in my heart. I must sit alone with
God, where I only listen to my sea of trouble.
I do not tackle it. I'm not in it.

The sea is lovely when it has borders.
That is when I see its beauty,
Hear its constant rhythm, and even admire its power.

THE EBB TIDE

In the name and in the strength
Of the King of Life,

In the name and in the strength
Of the Christ of Love,

In the name and in the strength
Of the Spirit of Guidance,

I cross the cold sea floor on
Dry ground.

The waters cannot touch me
Because the moon,

Servant of the glorious Creator,
Commands them to recede.

ADAPTED FROM *CARMINA GADELICA*

THE RESCUE BOX

If I wait too long to go to my island of solitude,
If I wait too long to cross the tidal flats,
I'll get caught in the terror and chaos of the
Incoming tide. It comes in gently at first,
Barely noticeable. But once I'm caught off guard,
Lingering too long, its final rush is mercilessly
Fierce and fast. Its drowning powers will
Overwhelm and destroy me.

But there is a rescue box – on stilts high above the causeway –
That I can climb to. There in that tiny cubicle, with the waters
Surging all around, is God and safety and calm.

TOURIST-TIDES

During the summer months,
There are two competing tides:
As the ebb tide retreats to the deep ocean,
The tourist-tide floods in from the mainland.
People come across the causeway: hundreds every day.
The island is not so quiet when they are here.
This tide leaves its mark.

Just when I think to settle into the
Solitude of Holy Island,
Cut off from the rush of the world,
The world comes to me.
All these people, looking for peace.
They will find it here;
I must invite them onto my island
So that they can carry its peace
Back home again.

The tide returns from the sea, flooding in.
Just so, the tourist-tide ebbs –
Rushing home
To the mainland,
Crossing just ahead of the waves,
Toting its island peace.

TIDE OF BUSYNESS

God of all calm,
Rescue me when I am
Overwhelmed with busyness.

There is a busyness that comes unbidden.
It seeps in slowly at first,
Through the foundation walls of my days,
Then rises until there is no stopping it.

There is a busyness that
Rushes in like a flood,
Because I have opened the sea-wall.
Suddenly I am drowning.

Be my ark, O God,
Until the waters dry up.
When I emerge,
Remind me that you
Promised to never again
Cover the world with water –
So why should I?

THE EVER-RETURNING GUEST

I sip my morning tea on Holy Island,
Free of care and fear.
You and I, Great Three of Love,
Together.

You speak, and the sea, my ever-returning guest,
Backs slowly and quietly from the scene,
Bowing and excusing herself with mannerly pretence:
Pardon me; just stepping away for a moment.
In actual fact, she is retreating to the ocean's depths,
Fleeing the sound of your voice,
Afraid of facing the One who defeats chaos.

Oh, she will be back.
Later, when she thinks you've left.
It's the sneaking in that's so maddening:
No big entrance, no announcement, but suddenly
There she is, just when our picnic tea is served.
Then she rushes in, swamping everything in the way,
Voracious, belching, howling about her appetite.

She sees you, sitting majestically at the head of
The table. How startled she is! Why does she not know,
After all these years, that you live here? Her thinly disguised
Act begins again (Ahem; must have a fish bone in my
Throat; please excuse me; sorry to have to leave) as she
Demurs and backs away.

Does she never grow tired of all this coming and going?

PRAYER AT RISING

Bless to me, O God,
Each thing mine eye sees;
Bless to me, O God,
Each sound mine ear hears;
Bless to me, O God,
Each odour that goes to my nostrils;
Bless to me, O God,
Each taste that goes to my lips;
Each note that goes to my song,
Each ray that guides my way,
Each thing that I pursue,
Each lure that tempts my will,
The zeal that seeks my living soul,
The Three that seek my heart,
The zeal that seeks my living soul,
The Three that seek my heart.

<small>CARMINA GADELICA</small>

Night Prayer

My God and my Chief,
I seek you in the morning,
My God and my Chief,
I seek you this night.
I give you my mind,
I give you my will,
I give you my wish,
My soul everlasting and my body.

Be shepherd over me,
Be guardian unto me,
Be herdsman over me,
Be guide unto me,
Be with me, O Chief of chiefs,
Father everlasting and God of the heavens.

ADAPTED FROM *CARMINA GADELICA*

THE EBB AND FLOW

As it was,
As it is,
As it shall be
Evermore,
O Thou Triune
Of grace!
With the ebb,
With the flow,
O Thou Triune
Of grace!
With the ebb,
With the flow.

CARMINA GADELICA

III
BOATS

7

REACHING SHORE

When evening came, his disciples went down to the sea, got into a boat, and started across the sea to Capernaum. It was now dark, and Jesus had not yet come to them. The sea became rough because a strong wind was blowing. When they had rowed about three or four miles, they saw Jesus walking on the sea and coming near the boat, and they were terrified. But he said to them, 'It is I; do not be afraid.' Then they wanted to take him into the boat, and immediately the boat reached the land toward which they were going.
JOHN 6:16–21

In this story from John's Gospel, Jesus' disciples are rowing across the Sea of Galilee when a great storm comes up. They have gone three to four miles, which John's readers would have recognized as exactly halfway across, too far to turn back. It is very, very dark; and Jesus, the light of the world, is absent. The men are caught and powerless.

We cannot help but return to the opening lines of Genesis chapter one: 'In the beginning God created the heavens and the earth. Now the earth was formless and empty, darkness was over the surface of the deep, and the Spirit of God was hovering over the waters.' It is an apt description of the unfamiliar and fearful place into which the disciples have fallen. They are literally in the middle of a dark, chaotic, primordial sea; but then, out of nowhere, Jesus appears, hovering over the waters. Wonder of wonders, the sea is in subjection to him – because he made it. He speaks: 'It is I; do not be afraid.' His words imply that fear gripped them, and not merely fear of the storm, but fear of this figure inexplicably walking on top of the lawless waves. How well they knew the ancient storm images in the Old Testament: Rahab, the Boisterous One; Leviathan, the hideous serpent of the deep; and the dreadful dragons with writhing tails. Is that who was coming towards them on the sea? As soon as Jesus speaks, however, their terror dissipates: 'It is I.' This is the name of the God of the Israelites – Yahweh, maker of sea and land and all that is; the I Am; the One Who Exists. When they hear these words, the disciples instantly want to take Jesus into their tiny boat.

When Matthew tells this same story in his Gospel, he concentrates on the courageous Peter – who jumps out of the boat and also walks on the water, until he loses his focus on Jesus, allows terror to seize him and begins to sink. Jesus grabs Peter, and together they climb on board. John's emphasis is different. In his account, all twelve disciples, not just Peter, act with great courage, because together they make a decision and a request: 'O God, get in our boat.' Such an intrepid move! They are, after all, in the darkness of a great gale. Surely each of them asks himself, 'What if that is *not* Jesus approaching us?' And then again, 'What if it *is* Jesus? Look at what he's doing: walking on water! What might he do next?' But his words reassure them: 'I Am.' They long, desperately, for him to get into their craft. And when he does, 'immediately the boat reached the land toward which they were going'. Suddenly they are on dry ground. The point of this story is not just that Jesus walks on water, as amazing as that is. Even more amazing is what happens when the frightened disciples take him into their boat. For that is the moment when Jesus separates sea from land. He removes the disciples from the dark waters and instantly deposits them on a safe shore. This is the Sign of Creation: God puts boundaries on sea and forms earth. It is the Sign of Noah: when the sea of un-creation flooded in on the world, God brought the ark through the deluge and the world started afresh, on

MY CURRACH

My currach ferries me across the strait,
Despite the dreadful monsters of the deep.
Enraged, they toss her high upon the swells,
Though through her seams the waters never seep.

But even so, I fear my barque will fail
As dark descends and now the gale grows fierce;
Yet still she battles on through crest and trough,
No storm her sturdy confidence can pierce.

Twelve fisher-folk appear, who ply the oars.
Now in the bow stands one who strode the waves.
He stretches forth his hand and speaks, 'Be still!'
The sea falls calm, the strident wind behaves.

Fast to my island home my craft makes speed,
As if the sea were land, my boat a steed.

dry ground. It is the Sign of Jonah: after nearly perishing in the sea, and spending three days in the formless abyss, God gives him a new start on dry land. That is what happens to the disciples on the Sea of Galilee. God gets in their little boat and immediately they are delivered from the deadly waves. Creation is all about driving back the untameable, swamping sea. God made us for land, and land is what John, the author of Revelation, saw in his vision of the new Eden to come: land, with no sea at all.

This miracle of Jesus walking on the sea during the storm is not for the crowds, who seek to be entertained by the latest ideas. It is for those who are in terror on the deep. It is for those who are inundated by the waves, wondering if they will ever make it home. God approaches us, and we say things like, 'Maybe it's a ghost!' Or, 'What if God harms me?' Or, 'What if God does something crazy?' Then we remember this story of the brave disciples and how Jesus came to them on the waves and saved them from the storm. He does not stand on the shore watching us from afar as we suffer in dark and  dangerous seas. He does not shout faint words of encouragement or try to throw us a life jacket. Jesus steps into the storm with us – right into its heart. He *hovers over* that black, formless void, just as he did in the beginning. He says, 'It is I. Let me create you anew.' Our weak hearts gain courage and we shout, 'O God, get in my boat!' And the moment God steps into our little currachs, Genesis chapter one happens in our lives: God puts a boundary on the sea and the storm, and sets us safely and forever on dry, solid ground.

Text Acknowledgments

pp. 15, 17, 18, 19, 23, 25, 43, 48–9, 63, 64, 77, 92 Scripture quotations are from the New Revised Standard Version published by HarperCollins Publishers, copyright © 1989 by the Division of Christian Education of the National Council of the Churches of Christ in the USA, and are used by permission. All rights reserved.
pp. 10–12 Shipwreck story adapted by Joyce Denham from Acts 27 of the New Revised Standard Version.
p. 54 'Colmcille' by John Montague. From the Irish, 6th century (?). By kind permission of the author c/o The Gallery Press, Loughcrew, Oldcastle, County Meath, Ireland.

Picture Acknowledgments

p. 1 copyright © Digital Vision
pp. 2–3 copyright © Brian Harris Editorial Photographer / Alamy
pp. 4–5 copyright © Nick Rous / Lion Hudson
p. 9 copyright © Goodshoot / Alamy
p. 14 copyright © Jeff Minter / Alamy
p. 22 copyright © Chris Hill / The Irish Image Collection
p. 27 copyright © David Lyons / Alamy
pp. 30–31 copyright © nagelestock.com / Alamy
p. 32 copyright © Nick Rous / Lion Hudson
pp. 36–37 copyright © Nigel Hicks / Alamy
p. 41 copyright © Boating Images Photo Library / Alamy
p. 43 copyright © Bernard Hymmen
p. 48 copyright © David Lyons / Alamy
p. 53 copyright © Nick Rous / Lion Hudson
p. 56 copyright © Jeff Minter / Alamy
p. 62 copyright © Eye Ubiquitous / Alamy
pp. 66–67 copyright © Simon Fraser / Alamy
p. 69 copyright © Nick Rous / Lion Hudson
p. 70 copyright © Gordon Chambers / Alamy
p. 74 copyright © Gary Cook / Alamy
p. 78 copyright © Leslie Garland Picture Library / Alamy
pp. 82–83 copyright © Don Brownlow / Alamy
p. 87 copyright © David Tipling / Alamy
pp. 90–91 copyright © Jeff Minter / Alamy
p. 95 copyright © Boating Images Photo Library / Alamy